THE ULTIMATE
BOOK OF
INCREDIBLE
EYE-TWISTERS

THE ULTIMATE BOOK OF INCREDIBLE EYE-TWISTERS

metro

Published by Metro Publishing Ltd,
3, Bramber Court, 2 Bramber Road,
London W14 9PB, England

www.blake.co.uk

First published in paperback in 2004

ISBN 1 84358 098 5

British Library Cataloguing-in-Publication Data:

A catalogue record for this book is available from the British Library.

Design by www.envydesign.co.uk

Printed in Great Britain by Clowes, Suffolk

1 3 5 7 9 10 8 6 4 2

Text copyright Metro Publishing 2004

Papers used by Metro Publishing are natural, recyclable products made from wood grown in sustainable forests. The manufacturing processes conform to the environmental regulations of the country of origin.

Every attempt has been made to contact the relevant copyright-holders, but some were unobtainable. We would be grateful if the appropriate people could contact us.

A percentage of profits from the book will be donated to the Sightsavers Charity.

Read the sign.

Now read it again.

Were you right the first time?

A
Bird
In The
The Bush

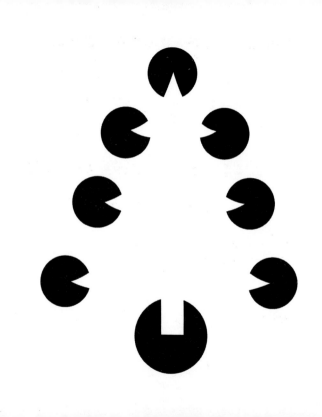

Is that a tree you see, or is it just your imagination?

Is there a triangle here, or are you seeing something that simply isn't there?

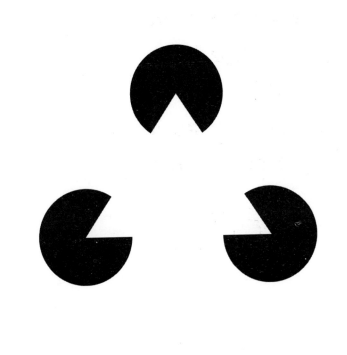

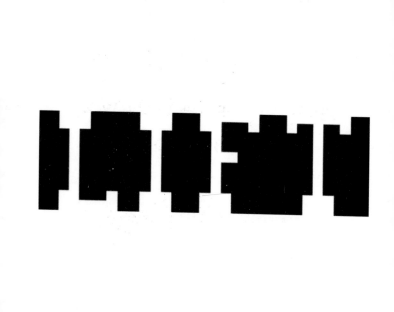

Sometimes the right word
can be hard to find.
Look at these shapes – is there
a hidden message?

Focus your eyes in a certain
direction to see this one!

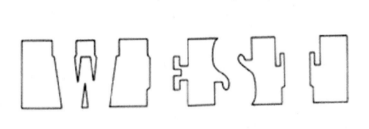

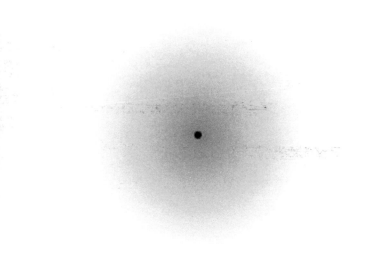

Things can't just disappear, can they? Stare at the black dot for a minute and think again!

Eye-Twisters

Project Charlie Chaplain onto your own small screen.
Stare at the white cross for a minute, then move your eyes to the black cross.

Do you believe in ghosts? Help this lost soul haunt a house by staring at him for a minute, then look at the arch. Spooky!

Spot the dog. Stare at the dot for a minute, then close your eyes. What do you see?

Here Kitty! Stare at the
dot for a minute, then shut your
eyes. Is there something in
the darkness?

Eye-Twisters

One for a rainy day.
Stare at the dot for a minute,
then close your eyes.

Eye-Twisters

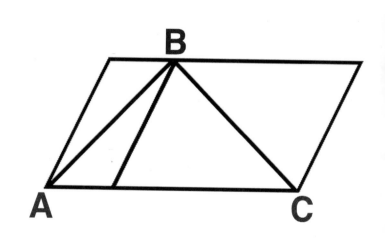

Which line is longer,
A-B or B-C?

Eye-Twisters

The shape at the bottom is bigger, isn't it?

Eye-Twisters

Impossible shapes, possibly.
Opposites, maybe. See for
yourself!

Eye-Twisters

Look at these still squares and circles. Could they be moving?

Eye-Twisters

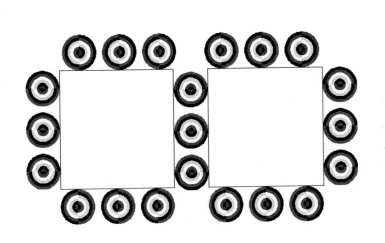

These half moons appear
different. Are they?

Eye-Twisters

Are these lines parallel?

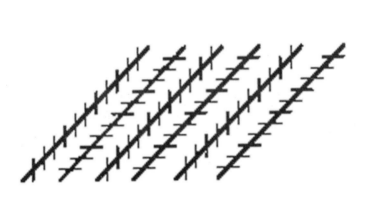

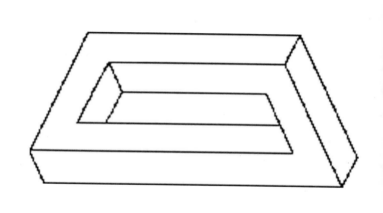

What exactly do we have here?

Is there more to these lines
than meets the eye?

Eye-Twisters

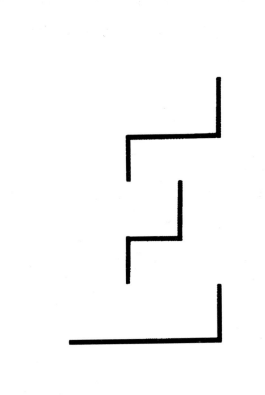

There's something odd about these interlocking rings? Can you tell what it is?

Eye-Twisters

Which surface is closest to you?

How many levels does this 3D image have? Don't let your eyes deceive you!

Eye-Twisters

Is it possible that the three prongs are on the same level?

Eye-Twisters

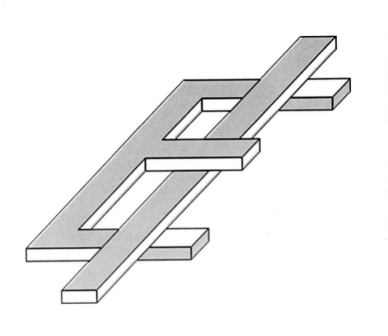

More interlocking shapes. How confusing!

Eye-Twisters

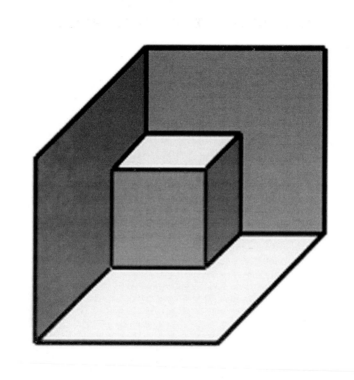

Is there a chunk missing from this box, or are there two boxes?

Eye-Twisters

Look at the top lines of these
simple shapes.
Which one is longer?

Eye-Twisters

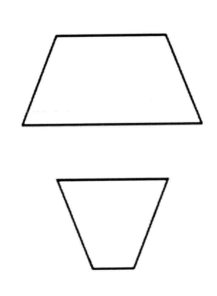

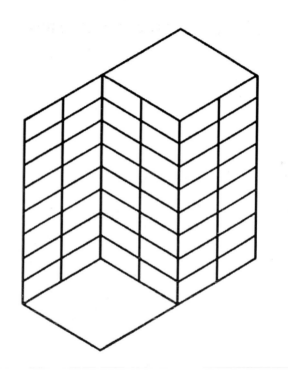

It is hard to say which way this
object is facing!

This one might send you
a bit dotty!

Move your head towards
the pattern, then move back.
Amazing!

This tyre appears to be moving.
Focus on the cross and
bring your face slowly towards
the image. Now move back –
freaky!

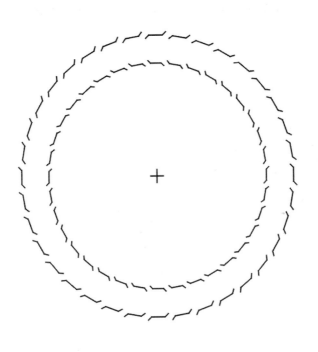

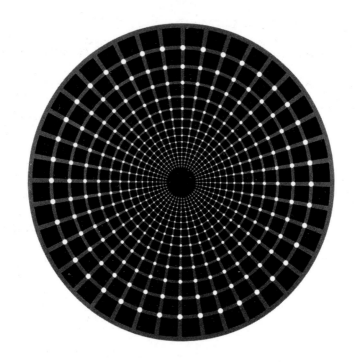

Circle your eyes around this pattern. Is there something odd about those 'white' dots?

Eye-Twisters

This one could make
you dizzy . . . steady!

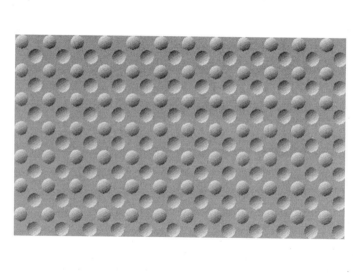

Focus on a point behind the page, then bring the image close to your face and relax your eyes. The balls begin to float.

Look at the circle and move
your head around.

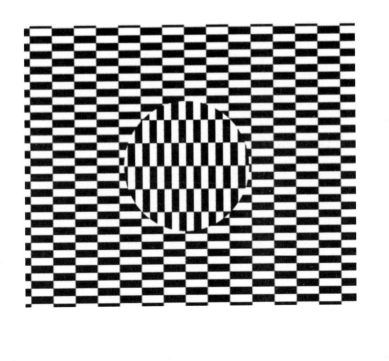

Focus on the centre of the image and move your head around.

Funny how these straight lines
appear to be curved!

Eye-Twisters

How many figures and faces
can you find?

Amazingly, these lines
are straight.

Eye-Twisters

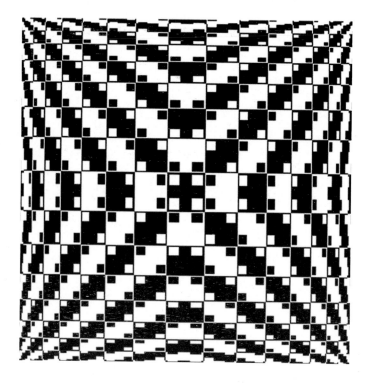

This cushion looks very comfortable, yet it has no curves at all.

Another impossible shape!

Eye-Twisters

Focus on the centre, and let this pattern bamboozle your eyes!

Eye-Twisters

Would these instructions be helpful to you?

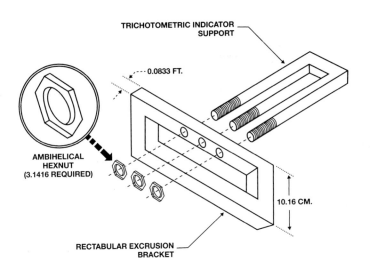

TRICHOTOMETRIC INDICATOR
SUPPORT

0.0833 FT.

AMBIHELICAL
HEXNUT
(3.1416 REQUIRED)

10.16 CM.

RECTABULAR EXCRUSION
BRACKET

Who'd have thought that a squirrel and a swan could be so closely related?

Eye-Twisters

Look carefully at this silhouette.
Which way is the horse facing?

Is this one woman, or twins. It's hard to tell the difference!

Don't let this one leave you
cold. Look carefully – what do
you see?

SIGMUND FREUD

Does this man have something
on his mind?

Smiling young man or
bearded old grump?
Turn the image upside down

They say that beauty is in
the eye of the beholder.
Can you see any here?

It's written all over his face!

100

Quite a tricky one, but it doesn't take Einstein to 'figure' this one out . . .

Are you sure there is a woman
in this picture?

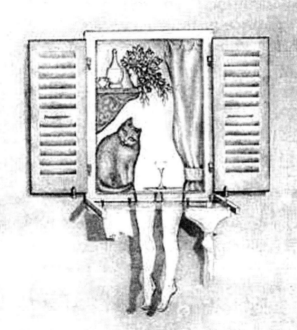

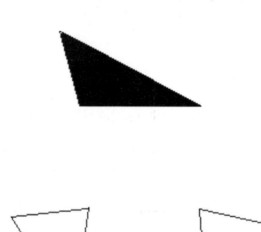

The king lives! Is there a hint of Elvis in these triangles?

Youth and old age can't be combined, can they? Turn these images upside down.

Which is the tallest figure?

Another tricky one! Are we looking down or up at the girl in the window?

Crater or mountain? Turn the picture upside down.

114

Look at this photo of Bill Clinton and Al Gore. Actually they are both Bill Clinton – one of them just has Al Gore's hair!

What a strange building 'sight'!

Cowboys – is this picture big enough for both of them!

Eye-Twisters